MOSQUITOES

For a free color catalog describing Gareth Stevens' list of high-quality books and multimedia programs, call 1-800-542-2595 (USA) or 1-800-461-9120 (Canada). Gareth Stevens Publishing's Fax: (414) 225-0377. See our catalog, too, on the World Wide Web: http://gsinc.com

Library of Congress Cataloging-in-Publication Data

Fisher, Enid.
    Mosquitoes / by Enid Broderick Fisher ; illustrated by Tony Gibbons.
      p. cm. -- (The New creepy crawly collection)
    Includes bibliographical references and index.
    Summary: Examines the anatomy, behavior, life cycle, and dangers of this
tiny member of the fly family.
    ISBN 0-8368-1916-0 (lib. bdg.)
    1. Mosquitoes--Juvenile literature. [1. Mosquitoes.] I. Gibbons, Tony, ill.
II. Title. III. Series.
QL536.F57 1997
595.77'2--dc21   97-7333

This North American edition first published in 1997 by
Gareth Stevens Publishing
1555 North RiverCenter Drive, Suite 201
Milwaukee, Wisconsin 53212 USA

This U.S. edition © 1997 by Gareth Stevens, Inc. Created with original © 1996 by Quartz Editorial Services, 112 Station Road, Edgware HA8 7AQ U.K.

Consultant: Matthew Robertson, Senior Keeper, Bristol Zoo, Bristol, England.

Printed in Mexico

1 2 3 4 5 6 7 8 9 01 00 99 98 97

THE NEW
CREEPY CRAWLY
COLLECTION

MOSQUITOES

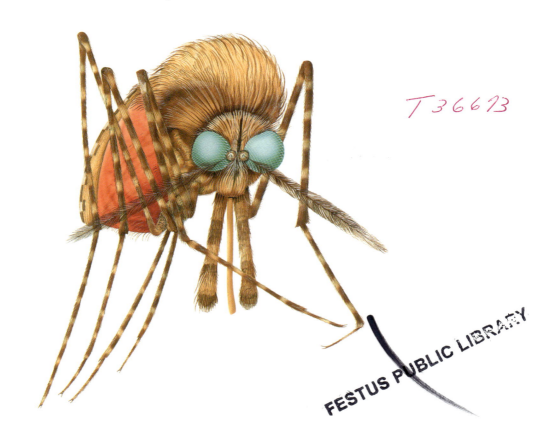

by Enid Broderick Fisher
Illustrated by Tony Gibbons

Gareth Stevens Publishing
MILWAUKEE

Contents

Getting to know mosquitoes

The weather is hot, and mosquitoes are out in force. Ouch! You've been bitten again. It's left a red bump and itches badly. But unless you're allergic to mosquito bites, the itching and swelling will go away in a few days.

Only a few of the three thousand different species of female mosquitoes can actually give you a serious illness if they bite you. Because of this, however, all mosquitoes have a bad name.

Mosquito is Spanish for "little fly," and that's exactly what they are — flies. Even though they are small, the females are like the vampires of the insect world.

Mosquitoes have some odd habits, too. For example, they lay their eggs in watery places and swarm at dusk. Females attract their mates with a loud buzzing of their beating wings.

Join us as we take a closer look at these tiny members of the fly family. They can be extremely annoying insects, as you will discover.

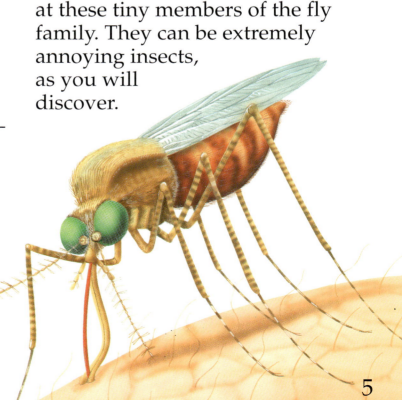

Bodywork

Under a microscope, you can see that the mosquito is about 0.3 inches (8 millimeters) long. It has two huge eyes that contain hundreds of tiny lenses that give it excellent eyesight. You can also see the two long antennae, or feelers, at the front of its head. A male's antennae (*right*) are covered with thousands of hairs and look like feathers, while a female has long, slender antennae. The mosquito uses these to feel its way along and also to sense if water is near.

Just look at the long spikes at the front of the female mosquito pictured on page 17! Only the female sucks blood, and she uses these needle-sharp spikes to feed on passing animals — and humans, too.

In contrast, the rest of the mosquito's body is pretty to observe. The colored marks on the abdomen are formed from scales that provide excellent camouflage. This way, predators will not spot them easily.

Mosquitoes come in many colors. Some are a plain brown that blends easily with a background of tree bark. Others have sporty black-and-white stripes that make them almost invisible in a forest's dappled shade.

The mosquito is called a "true" fly because it has two wings. These wings also have scales that shimmer in sunlight. The scales are transparent, so you can see right through them. The scales are made of membranes that are divided like stained-glass windows by black, thread-like veins.

The mosquito can also crawl around on its six long, spidery legs. These allow it to make a soft, silent landing on prey. The victim will probably be unaware that a female mosquito is there or may feel only a slight tickle — until it bites, of course!

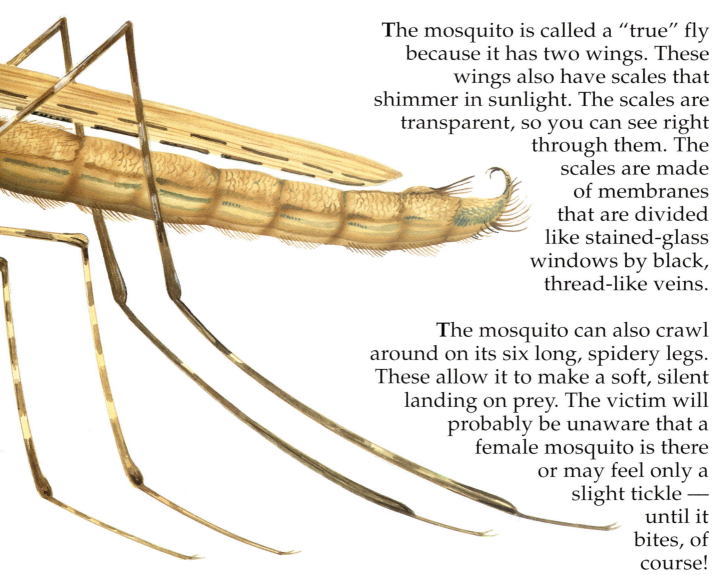

Creatures of the night

Lots of flies like light — but not most mosquitoes! They are nocturnal and prefer to hide until dark.

At sunset, *Culex* and *Anopheles* mosquitoes stir from their daytime rest, feeling very hungry. Suddenly, the night air is alive with female mosquitoes looking for victims to bite.

They are very greedy. In fact, scientists know that a single female mosquito can attack as many as eighteen people an hour. After they have been this active for a while, they then slow down to about five bites per hour until just before sunrise, when they increase their intake of blood once more.

In hot countries, where the mosquitoes carry malaria, many people put up a special net around their beds to protect them from mosquito bites while they sleep.

Having a bright light stay on all night also helps keep them away.

Not all mosquitoes come out at night. Forest mosquitoes of the *Aedes* and *Sabethe* species are diurnal, which means they come out during the day. They prefer the warmth of the sun to the cold of the night. They, too, are more likely to attack at sunrise and sunset; they need a blood-meal just after they wake up and again just before they go to sleep.

Noisy

Shhh! Can you hear that buzzing down by the pond? It will soon be dusk, and things should be quiet. So what's going on? Look through a pair of binoculars to find out.

A lot of flies are hovering just above the water. What an amazing sight! And they're not just any flies — they're mosquitoes! Better not go *too* close — female mosquitoes can suck blood! But it's all right. Most of these are males, and they can't suck blood. They don't buzz, either; so all that loud noise is coming from females.

swarms

There don't seem to be many of them. You wouldn't think that just a few insects could make so much noise, but those wings are beating the air at five hundred beats a second! The males are going wild. All this commotion is a mating game. Some types of male mosquitoes even swarm in a kind of dance to attract the females.

If they are interested in mating, the female mosquitoes won't be looking for someone to bite — not yet. But, later, those females will want a blood-meal before they lay their eggs — so that's the time to avoid them.

11

Meals of blood

Imagine for a moment that a mosquito can talk. It's a female with such light, thin legs that victims can hardly feel its slight tickle as it walks all over their skin.

"I'm hungry for a meal of blood, so I will start to open a big, furry spike on my head. It has six sharp points inside. These are my stylets, and I pierce my victim's skin with them.

"Just look at that big bump on his hand! It's red, and he can't stop scratching it. He'll have to put on some medicated cream to make it feel better.

"Luckily, I don't pass on diseases, unlike my terrible cousins, the dreaded *Anopheline* mosquitoes. They can make people very ill.

"Nevertheless, we are all regarded as the scourge of the human race, whether we cause illnesses like malaria or not. Everyone finds us a nuisance. That's because female mosquitoes like me can give people a nasty bite.

"We particularly like a meal of blood before we lay our eggs. Male mosquitoes, however, survive on plant juices and sap.

"Most of my victims only suffer a mild irritation at the spot where I pierce the skin. But some people develop a much more serious reaction to my bites, sometimes bad stomach pains or even vomiting. It is probably my saliva they are reacting to. It is injected into the victims as I suck up some of their delicious blood!"

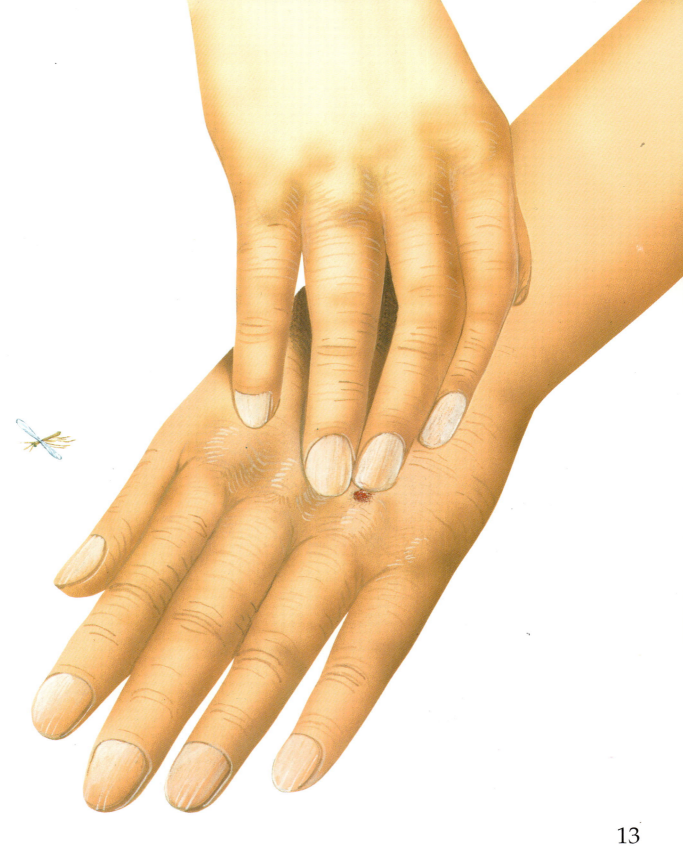

Life cycle

After they have mated, female mosquitoes fly to almost anyplace that has a few inches (cm) of water.

Most types of female mosquitoes need a blood-meal before they lay their eggs. *Culicine* mosquitoes lay up to three hundred eggs. They all stick together and float on the water.

Ponds or puddles, marshes or ditches — all of these places are ideal. If there is no stretch of water nearby, then swimming pools, watertubs, or old tin cans will do.

At this stage, the mass of eggs looks like a tiny raft that is only about 0.2 inches (5 mm) long, as seen enlarged *above*.

Anopheline mosquitoes however, lay about thirty single eggs, each with an outer shell that traps air and acts as a tiny float. This keeps the eggs from sinking to the bottom.

After a few days, each larva hatches through a trapdoor at the bottom of the egg and wriggles to the surface. *Culicine* larvae have a tube at their tail end to suck up air, so they all hang upside-down in a row, as shown *below, left*.

After about three weeks, the larvae develop into pupae. They have a curved shape, just like a comma, and they also wriggle around under the water surface. They will soon enter the next stage of development and change their appearance completely.

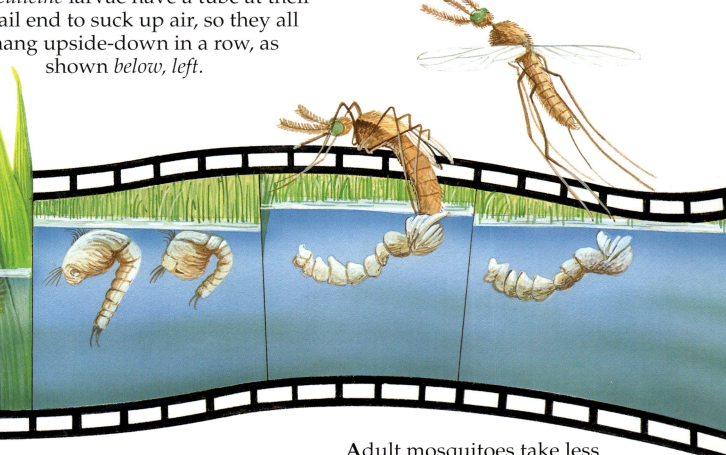

Anopheline larvae, however, have two trumpet-like tubes on their head. They lie flat under the water and use these tubes to breathe.

Adult mosquitoes take less than a week to emerge from the pupae, without even getting wet! Then they shake their wings and are ready to fly away.

15

Malaria

Imagine being in an unbearably hot room but feeling freezing cold. Then, suddenly, you can't stand the heat as your temperature soars to over 104° F (40° C). Your body is shaking, and your head aches.

You would feel like this if you had malaria. But, fortunately, there are drugs that can usually help in an attack. Even so, many people still die from malaria. It's one of the world's biggest killers.

You won't get malaria every time you are bitten by a mosquito. Only the *Anopheline* type, seen here, can infect you. It lives mainly in tropical regions, such as Africa, Southeast Asia, some Mediterranean countries, and South America.

A famous Greek doctor named Hippocrates knew that malaria existed as a disease as long ago as 400 B.C.

But it was not until 1897 that a scientist named Ronald Ross found that people get malaria from mosquito bites.

So how does the mosquito carry this disease? It sucks up parasites when biting someone who already has malaria. These parasites then breed inside the mosquito and infect its saliva. When the mosquito needs its next blood-meal, it pierces its new victim's skin and injects the infected saliva. The unfortunate, infected person soon becomes very ill.

Between 1700 and World War II (1939-45), malaria victims were treated with a medicine called quinine, which comes from the bark of the South American cinchona tree. Many lives were saved by using this medication.

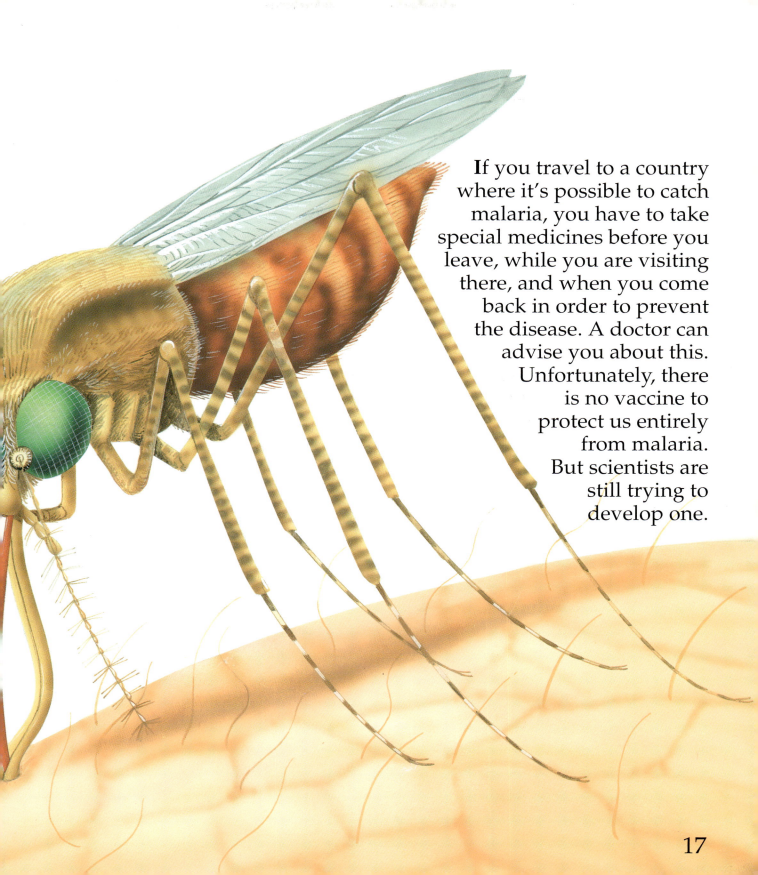

If you travel to a country where it's possible to catch malaria, you have to take special medicines before you leave, while you are visiting there, and when you come back in order to prevent the disease. A doctor can advise you about this. Unfortunately, there is no vaccine to protect us entirely from malaria. But scientists are still trying to develop one.

Habitats

Most of the world's mosquitoes live in tropical countries, where the climate is hot and humid. But some types can be found in cooler countries. A sturdy few can even survive the frozen wastes of Siberia, deep inside the Arctic Circle.

Tropical mosquitoes make their home in lush forests and jungles, as shown in the illustration *opposite*. In other countries, wooded areas provide suitable living quarters. Most mosquitoes prefer the hours of darkness, but some types can live in the shade of a leafy glade or the high canopy of trees.

Mosquitoes spend much of their time resting. This happens after they have had a blood-meal, just as some people enjoy a nap after a heavy lunch. During daylight hours, the nocturnal species hide in all sorts of dark corners.

Forest-dwelling mosquitoes, which feed on the blood of animals, creep into cracks in trees where their dappled coloring makes them almost invisible. Those that do not like light at all crawl under stones or into the sunless nooks and crannies of caves.

Mosquitoes that want meals of human blood, such as *Anophelus maculpennis* (which can pass on malaria), hide in dark supply or tool sheds or garages. Some will even come into the house and lurk under the stairs or in the attic.

A lot of mosquitoes live in areas near water. Still ponds, marshes, or swamps are the best places, but mosquitoes can also live near flowing rivers that have quiet pools along their banks. The water doesn't have to be clean, either.

War against

Every year, there are about 250 million cases of malaria reported worldwide, and about two million people die from it. Half of these are children who live in poor countries, and who are not usually in good health to begin with.

In the picture *opposite*, you can see how two malaria parasites (colored by the artist in blue and pink) have invaded a red blood cell after a bite from a malaria-carrying mosquito. This is what the infected blood cell looks like under a microscope, which has enlarged it several thousand times.

Mosquitoes can't be caught without the danger of their bites, so other ways are needed to get rid of them. Their breeding areas can be sprayed with chemicals called insecticides, such as DDT. This certainly kills off mosquitoes, but it is not the ideal answer to the problem.

After twenty years of spraying mosquito breeding grounds in Sri Lanka, for example, there were only eighteen reported cases of malaria. But five years later, half a million people caught the disease. This happened because the mosquitoes became resistant to the effect of insecticides.

Many countries have also banned some insecticides because they destroy other insects and wildlife, and can even harm humans.

Another way of getting rid of mosquitoes is to destroy their habitats, which are mainly watery places. Draining swamps and lakes, and filling in marshes with tons of earth has drastically reduced the mosquito population in some countries. Once again, though, this can destroy other harmless creatures simply by the unnatural reorganization of their natural environment.

mosquitoes

In some poorer countries, people try to raise their standard of living by irrigating the desert to grow crops. This sometimes creates new breeding grounds for mosquitoes, causing new problems. At this time, humans do not seem to be winning the war against mosquitoes.

One idea, however, that scientists have come up with is to introduce a special fish into the lakes where mosquitoes are known to breed. This type of fish loves to eat mosquito larvae and so helps to keep the mosquito population down.

Not surprisingly, it is known as the mosquito-fish, a type of minnow. This method seems fairly promising, and it is environmentally safe.

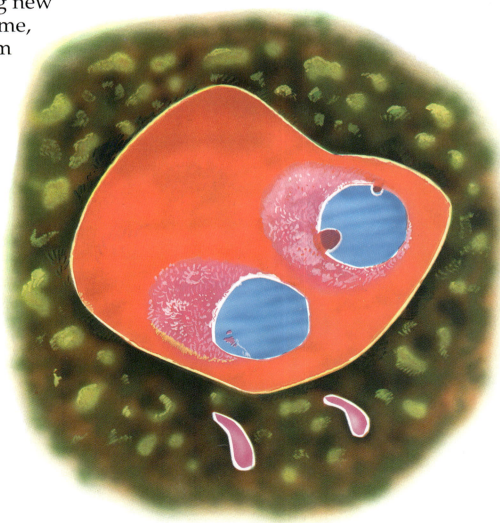

Did you know?

▼ *Do mosquitoes have any enemies?*
Adult mosquitoes can be trapped by spiders in their webs, just like other flying insects, and as seen *below*. The larvae and pupae, which spend all their time under water, are also caught by birds as well as other aquatic creatures, such as fish, frogs, and newts.

How can humans avoid being bitten by a mosquito?
You can buy insect repellent to rub or spray on your skin. This is unpleasant for the mosquito that wants to land on you. And, if you live in a tropical area that is plagued by mosquitoes, you can use a mosquito net at night.

How long do mosquitoes live?
Male mosquitoes live for only about two or three weeks. Females, however, can survive for several months. They can even hibernate over winter or during cold weather.

Can mosquitoes carry diseases other than malaria?
The same mosquitoes that carry malaria can also pass on other diseases, such as elephantiasis, which causes parts of the body to swell up to a huge size. The Egyptian mosquito, *Aedes aegypti*, can pass on yellow fever to a human victim.

▲ Do mosquitoes eat anything else besides blood?

Female mosquitoes can suck nectar from flowers and juice from fruits, as well as blood from animals and humans. Male mosquitoes, however, have no piercing mouthparts, so they do not suck blood. They exist on nectar and plant juices only.

Can you identify malaria-carrying mosquitoes from other types?

If you look at an *Anopheline* mosquito when it is standing still, you will recognize it because its bottom sticks up in the air. *Culicine* mosquitoes, which do not spread malaria, hold their bodies level and bend their heads down.

Is it true that mosquitoes steal honeydew from ants?

Some ants take tiny droplets of honeydew (a sugary substance) from aphids. When the ants carry away their booty, mosquitoes may land in front of them, batting their wings rapidly up and down. This hypnotizes the ants, whose jaws drop open. Quick as a flash, the mosquitoes' mouthparts dart inside the ants' mouths, and they steal the honeydew. What clever robbers!

Can you catch malaria from a human or another type of insect?

You can only catch malaria as a result of a bite from a malaria-carrying mosquito. Malaria is carried only by the mosquito and no other animals. Humans cannot usually pass on malaria.

Do mosquitoes attack only people?

Mosquitoes will attack any creature that can supply them with blood, including rats, monkeys, apes, birds, and reptiles. But certain species of mosquitoes tend to attack the same types of victims.

Glossary

antennae — movable sensory organs, or feelers, on the head of an insect that are used for touching and smelling.

camouflage — markings or coloring that help an animal or plant disguise itself and blend in with its natural environment.

diurnal — active during the day.

larva — the wingless stage of an insect's life cycle between egg and pupa.

malaria — a disease spread by mosquitoes. People with malaria have chills, fever, and sweating.

mate (v) — to join (animals) together to produce young.

nocturnal — active at night.

predators — animals that hunt and kill other animals for food.

pupa — the stage of an insect's life between larva and adult.

quinine — a bitter medicine used to treat malaria.

species — animals or plants that are closely related and often similar in behavior or appearance. Members of the same species can breed together.

stylet — a sharp, pointed, piercing organ or body part.

Books and Videos

Insects. Under the Microscope series. John Woodward (Gareth Stevens)

Mosquito! Angel Nieto (Scholastic)

Mosquitoes. Dorothy H. Patent (Holiday)

Flies and Mosquitoes: Their Life Cycle and Control. (Encyclopædia Britannica Educational Corp. video)

Insects Harmful to Man. (International Film Bureau)

The Mosquito: A Bite for Survival. (Encyclopædia Britannica Educational Corporation video)

Index